LEARN ABOUT

MAGNETS

STEVE PARKER

LORENZ BOOKS

This edition is published by Lorenz Books, an imprint of
Anness Publishing Ltd, Hermes House, 88–89 Blackfriars Road,
London SE1 8HA; tel. 020 7401 2077; fax 020 7633 9499

www.lorenzbooks.com; www.annesspublishing.com

If you like the images in this book and would like to investigate using
them for publishing, promotions or advertising, please visit our website
www.practicalpictures.com for more information.

UK agent: The Manning Partnership Ltd; tel. 01225 478444; fax 01225
478440; sales@manning-partnership.co.uk
UK distributor: Grantham Book Services Ltd; tel. 01476 541080; fax
01476 541061; orders@gbs.tbs-ltd.co.uk
North American agent/distributor: National Book Network; tel. 301 459
3366; fax 301 429 5746; www.nbnbooks.com
Australian agent/distributor: Pan Macmillan Australia; tel. 1300 135 113;
fax 1300 135 103; customer.service@macmillan.com.au
New Zealand agent/distributor: David Bateman Ltd; tel. (09) 415 7664;
fax (09) 415 8892

Publisher: Joanna Lorenz
Editor: Sam Batra
Consultant: Alison Porter, BSc, Science Museum, London
Photographer: John Freeman
Stylists: Thomasina Smith and Isolde Sommerfeldt
Designer: Caroline Reeves
Picture Researcher: Liz Eddison
Illustrator: Kuo Kang Chen

ETHICAL TRADING POLICY
Because of our ongoing ecological investment programme, you, as our
customer, can have the pleasure and reassurance of knowing that a tree is
being cultivated on your behalf to naturally replace the materials used to
make the book you are holding. For further information about this
scheme, go to www.annesspublishing.com/trees

The Publishers would like to thank the following children from St John
the Baptist Church of England School and Walnut Tree Walk Primary
School – Danny Bill, Katie Blue, Tony Borg, Stephen Grimshaw, Lauren
Kendrick, Sharday Manahan, Mikki Melaku, Yew Hong Mo, Nickolas
Moore, Louise Morgan, Lola Olayinka, Yemisi Omolewa, Stephen Reid,
Gemma Turland, Joe Westbrook, also Sophie and Alex Lindblom-Smith.
Thanks to Caroline Beattie, the Early Learning Centre, London and
Broadhurst, and Clarkson and Fuller, London.

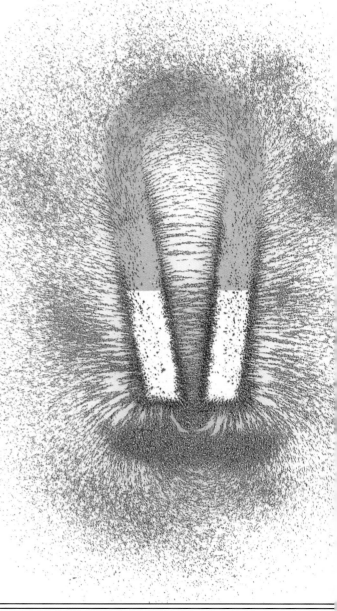

MAGNETS

CONTENTS

MAGNETS AND MAGNETISM

A magnet inside a colourful plastic case can hold pieces of paper on metal surfaces such as those of a fridge or washing machine. Enjoy rearranging them as often as you like.

Have you used a magnet today? Perhaps you fixed a message on the fridge door with a magnetic note-holder. Magnets and magnetism are found in many other places too. Almost any device or machine that has an electric motor uses magnetism – from a cassette tape-player or CD player, to a washing machine or tumble-dryer. Countless other bits of equipment and machinery also use magnetism, in the home, school, office and factory. They include computers, radios, power drills, and even giant electricity-making power stations. Magnetism is still a mysterious force that cannot be seen. Yet we live with its effects every day.

Speed
Are there magnets on bicycles? Some bicycles have a speedometer that works with a spinning magnet. If the bicycle's lights are powered by a dynamo, that also uses magnetism.

A warm blow
The electric motor in a hair-dryer uses magnetism. It spins a small fan that blows warm air at you and dries your hair.

Finding the way
Today boats and ships have satellite navigation systems. However, they still use a magnetic compass to check their route and find the way, just like sailors did hundreds of years ago.

Making music
To create its sound, the electric guitar relies on magnetism to make electrical signals. The guitar is plugged into an electric amplifier so that its sound can be heard.

Flying high
Modern aircraft have magnetic compasses and many of their dials, systems and equipment use magnetism. Magnets also let the pilots take a rest as they are used in the autopilot that controls the plane for part of the journey.

WHAT IS A MAGNET?

Magnets are usually made of the metal iron, or another metal that has lots of iron in it, such as steel. They can be various shapes, big or small, but all magnets have a curious ability that seems almost magical. They can pull things towards themselves by an invisible force called magnetism. But a magnet only attracts, or pulls, certain things, mainly those that are made of iron, or contain iron.

A magnet's power to attract can be transferred through objects. To see this, attach a steel paper-clip on to a magnet. Then hang another paper-clip on to the first and so on to make a chain.

Making magnet metal
Most magnets are made from iron or steel that contains iron. The raw materials come from ore or rocks with iron in them. These are heated until they melt.

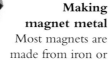

Shape and size
You cannot tell magnets by their shape or size. They can be straight bars, buttons, horseshoes and many other shapes. They may be red, but that is just paint to make them look good. This is a horseshoe magnet. Magnets are often shaped like this.

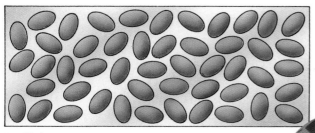
Jumbled-up micro-magnets.

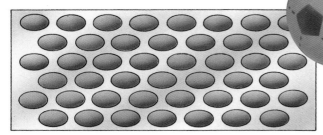
Lined-up micro-magnets.

Tiny magnets

Think of a bar of iron as having millions of micro-magnets inside it, called domains. If these are all jumbled up, the bar is not a magnet. If the micro-magnets in a bar are lined up and point the same way, it is a magnet.

Atoms

The tiny domains, or micro-magnets, inside iron are actually groups of atoms. All materials – metals, non-metals, gases and liquids – are made from atoms, which are so small that even the most powerful microscopes cannot see them. Atoms spin round and round, just like a ball balanced on the top of your finger.

FACT BOX

• You cannot tell if something is a magnet simply by looking at its shape, size or colour. You need to test it with objects that contain iron.

• Ordinary types of magnets are called permanent magnets. They are magnetic all the time and they keep their magnetism for months and years. There are other kinds of magnets, such as electromagnets, whose strength and magnetism can be varied.

• Every magnet has two poles or ends, no matter what shape it is.

• Most metals are not magnetic. The most common magnetic metals are cobalt, nickel and iron.

MAKING MAGNETS

Y OU can make your own magnet from a rod, strip or bar of something made of iron or steel that is not already a magnet. To do this, you also need a ready-made magnet. There are many suitable items, from screws to screwdrivers. Try some objects that are made from different metals, like brass or aluminium, or from other substances such as wood, plastic or paper. See what you discover when you experiment with these other materials, and then compare your conclusions with the findings made when iron or steel is used.

You will need: an iron nail, magnet, paper-clips, brass pin.

A simple horseshoe magnet is a familiar but fascinating object.

Your own magnet

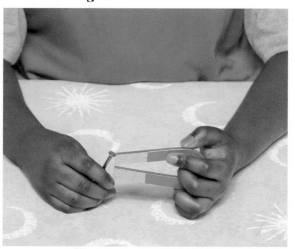

Take an iron nail and stroke it about 50 times with one end of a ready-made magnet. Stroke it along its length from one end to the other. The nail is now a magnet itself. Can it pick up a paper-clip or a brass pin?

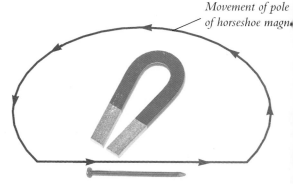

Movement of pole of horseshoe magnet

This diagram shows how to move the magnet when stroking the nail. Remember to always use the same pole, to move in the same direction and to lift the magnet clear after each stroke.

Does it stick?
Objects made of brass or other metals, apart from iron or steel, cannot usually be made into magnets. Do they even stick to a proper magnet?

Ruining a magnet
Use the iron nail that you have made into a magnet. Carefully tap it hard several times with the hammer. This shakes up all the tiny micro-magnets inside and destroys the magnetism.

M A T E R I A L S

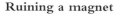

You will need: brass screw, magnet, iron nail, hammer, empty aluminium drinks can, paper-clip.

Testing magnets
The usual test for a magnet is to try and pick up something made of iron or steel. If an iron nail is too heavy for a weak magnet, try a shiny steel paper-clip instead.

Non-magnetic metal
The drinks can is aluminium. It does not stick to a proper magnet. You cannot make it into a magnet by stroking, either, no matter how long you might try!

HISTORY OF MAGNETS

P EOPLE have known about magnets and magnetism for thousands of years. This is because some magnets occur naturally. In certain places, you can pick them up from the ground. These natural magnets usually come in the form of lumps of stone called lodestone or magnetite, a type of rock that contains lots of iron. Ancient peoples noticed that two lumps of this rock might try to stick together. Then sailors and explorers discovered how to use thin slivers of this rock as magnetic compasses to find their way. However, people have only understood more about magnets in the last 200 years.

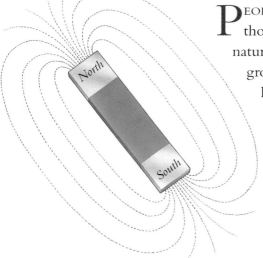

A typical bar magnet has two ends called poles. The invisible magnetism, called lines of magnetic force, are strongest around these ends.

The compass
About 1,000 years ago, sailors and explorers made a discovery. They found that a thin piece of lodestone, floating freely in a bowl of water, would always point the same way - north and south. They had discovered the magnetic compass.

Magnetic rock
Lodestone, also called magnetite, is a natural magnet. Dig it out of the ground and iron-containing objects such as nails and pins stick to it — just as they do to manufactured magnets.

Compass on board

During the great days of sailing ships, the magnetic compass was a vital piece of equipment. It showed which way was north, south, east or west. The navigator used the compass and maps to follow the ship's position.

Better compasses

In the 1600s compasses were being made using strips of magnetized iron, which were allowed to twirl around freely. The compass was put in an elegant, portable box that was decorated with attractive designs and patterns.

The fabled land

Some adventurers suggested that the North Pole, to which a magnetic compass points, was a paradise bathed in sunlight and peace. Others wanted to discover new trade routes by finding a way around the top of North America, as a short cut to the East. But their ships got trapped, their camps froze and many explorers died. The Magnetic north pole was first reached by British explorer James Ross and his expedition in 1831.

FACT BOX

• The name magnet may come from Magnesia. This was a region in Thessaly, in Ancient Greece. A part of modern Greece in the same area is called Magnisia.

• More than 2,500 years ago, the Ancient Greeks knew of the mysterious powers of the rock called lodestone.

• No one is sure who invented the first magnetic compass. It may have been the Ancient Chinese, about 1,800 years ago. By the year AD1000 the Chinese were using compasses to find their way at sea.

• By the AD1100s, the use of compasses had spread as far as the Middle East and Europe.

WHAT DO MAGNETS ATTRACT?

MOST ordinary magnets attract only certain objects. These are things containing the metal iron. So, how can you tell if an object is made of iron or contains iron? Try testing it with a magnet. For some objects the attraction is very weak, so you have to do this carefully and feel for the pulling force. For other objects, the attraction is strong enough to make them stick to the magnet. Remember that it is the magnet that does the pulling and not the object, unless that is a magnet too!

The human body has tiny amounts of iron in the blood, but too little to be affected by a magnet.

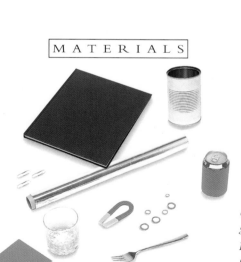

MATERIALS

Cans and tins
A fizzy-drinks can is probably made of aluminium. This is a metal, but it is not iron. The magnet does not pull or attract it. You could try an empty food tin, such as baked beans or soup. What happens then?

You will need: magnet, aluminium drinks can, empty food tin, plastic or glass beaker, stainless steel fork, book, paper, card, paper-clip, metal washers and aluminium cooking foil.

Paper, card and board

Try the magnetic test on a book or a sheet of paper. Does the magnet attract them? Can the magnetism attract a paper-clip? Will it pass through the book or paper? Try different thicknesses of these materials and note down your results.

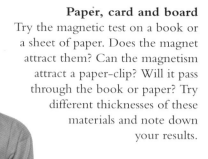

Glass and plastic

Try the beaker to see if the magnet attracts it. Glass and plastic do not contain iron, so they are not magnetic. See if the magnetism can pass through the beaker by holding the magnet on the outside and putting the fork on the inside.

Just passing through

Test metal washers with a magnet. They are probably steel, so they are attracted to it. Test cooking foil, too. It is probably aluminium, so it is not attracted. Now test the washers, with the foil between them and the magnet. Does the magnetism pass through the foil?

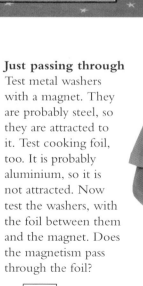

POLES APART

Some magnets, such as this bar magnet (left), have their different poles coloured or labelled. It is usually red or N for north. Another colour, sometimes blue, may represent S for south.

THE two poles, or ends, of a magnet may look the same, but they are not. Put one pole of a magnet near to a pole of another magnet to find out the differences. You may feel an attraction force, or pulling, as the two poles stick together strongly. Alternatively, you may feel a repulsion force, or pushing, as the two poles twist and repel each other. The different poles are called the north pole and the south pole. In all magnets two identical poles will push each other away, while two different poles will pull towards each other. These are basic features of all magnets.

Like poles repel
Like poles repel, unlike poles attract. This saying helps you to remember a vital feature about magnets. It means that poles that are the same will repel, or push each other apart. Put two north poles together, and they repel. Two south poles also repel.

Unlike poles attract

The poles of two magnets that are different, or opposite, will attract. Put a north pole and south pole together and they will attract.

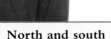

North and south

Why are a magnet's poles called north and south? This is because the north pole points to the Magnetic North Pole in the Arctic at the top of the world. The south pole points to the Magnetic South Pole on Antarctica. Their full names are north-seeking pole and south-seeking pole.

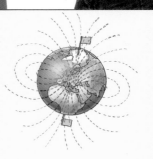

Poles and shapes

Magnetism is concentrated around the poles of a magnet. In the button-shaped note-holder magnets *(above)*, each pole is on an opposite side of the disc. This is why the magnet sticks to the fridge sideways-on.

Push-up train

Some trains have no wheels. Instead there are magnets in the base of the train and magnetism in the track. The like poles face each other, so they repel, lifting the train so it floats by magnetic repulsion. This is called magnetic levitation, or maglev.

SEEING MAGNETISM

YOU cannot see the magnetic force around a magnet. But you can see the effects of its presence when an iron nail sticks to a magnet. You can see the shape and extent of a magnetic field by using tiny, powder-like pieces of iron called iron filings. Magnetism makes them move and line up. More than 150 years ago, British scientist Michael Faraday studied magnets using iron filings. He noticed that the iron filings were lined up by lines of magnetic force. Today, diagrams are drawn to show that magnetism is made up of lines of magnetic force. The north pole has a + sign (positive or plus) and the south pole a – sign (negative or minus).

You cannot see magnetic lines of force. You cannot feel them, hear, smell or taste them. People need to use magnetic objects, like paper-clips, iron filings or a compass, to see how strong a magnetic force is.

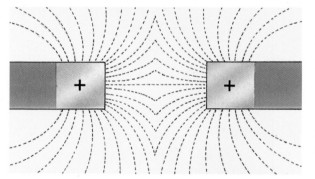

Repulsion force
Magnetic lines of force from the like poles of two magnets push against each other strongly. They can be north and north or south and south.

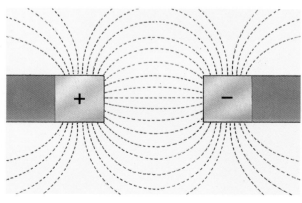

Attraction force
Magnetic lines of force from unlike poles – north and south – join and pull together powerfully. The attracting force is stronger than one magnet pulling on an ordinary iron object such as a nail.

Ring magnet
Iron filings are tiny and light. They can move about to line up with the magnetic force and they cluster where it is strongest. They show that this ring magnet has one pole on the inside of the ring and the other around the outside.

Compasses and magnetic fields

A magnetic compass usually lines up with the Earth's weak magnetism. Place a strong magnet nearby and you can overpower the Earth's magnetism and make the compass needle line up with it. However, the north end of the compass will point away from the magnet's north pole and the compass's south end from the magnet's south pole. The whole area of magnetism around any magnet, as shown by the lines of magnetic force, is called its magnetic field. Stronger magnets have bigger magnetic fields. The power of the magnetic field fades as it gets farther from its magnet.

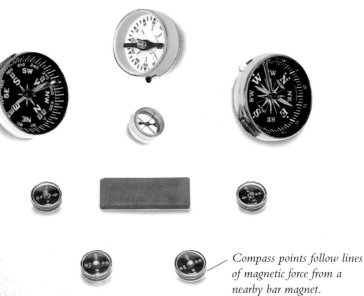

Compass points follow lines of magnetic force from a nearby bar magnet.

Bar magnet

Iron filings line up to show how the magnetic force spreads out from the poles, or ends of the bar. The tiny particles of filings are magnetic, but not magnetized, as they do not keep their magnetism when the bar magnet is removed.

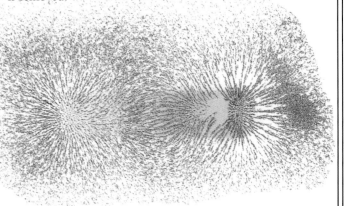

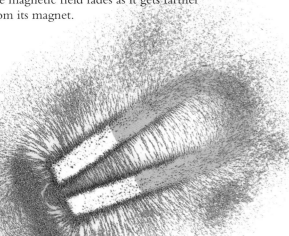

Horseshoe magnet

Iron filings reveal that the lines and strength of the magnetic force are concentrated around and between the poles at the ends of the horseshoe. There is little magnetism on the curved main body of the magnet because it is farther away from the poles.

PUSH AND PULL

You will need: scissors, sticky tape, round plastic container, 2 magnets, elastic bands, steel washers, ruler.

I s a big magnet more powerful than a small one? This is not necessarily the case because you cannot tell how powerful a magnet is just by looking at it. A magnet that is smaller than a matchbox can be stronger than one bigger than a housebrick. It depends on exactly what the magnet is made of, and how it is first given its magnetism or magnetized. Every year, vast amounts of money are spent on research into new combinations of metals to make magnets that are smaller, lighter and stronger than their predecessors. These combinations are called alloys, and steel, made from iron and carbon, is a common example. This simple magnet strength-tester compares the power of different magnets.

Strength of a magnet

1 Cut off a length of sticky tape and use it to fix the round container firmly to the work surface. This will act as the pivot, or the balancer.

2 Attach a magnet to one end of the ruler with an elastic band and some washers to the other end. Position the middle of the ruler on the balancer.

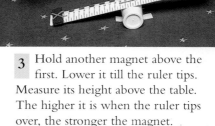

3 Hold another magnet above the first. Lower it till the ruler tips. Measure its height above the table. The higher it is when the ruler tips over, the stronger the magnet.

Power of a magnet

1 Using thread attached to a pin and a pencil, or compasses, draw two large quarter-circles on the card. The distance from the centre to the edge should be the ruler's length.

2 Draw a triangle in one quarter-circle and cut it out. Make a triangle from the second quarter-circle. Tape the two together, as above.

3 Push a drawing pin through the hole at the ruler's end so that it pivots. Attach elastic bands from the hole in the middle of the ruler to the quarter-circle's side, as shown. Add sticky dots to each end of the ruler and label them N and S.

You will need: thread, drawing pins, pencil, card, compasses, scissors, sticky tape, ruler with 2 holes in it, elastic bands, sticky dots, pen, magnets.

4 Stand the magnet-measurer upright. Fix one magnet to the ruler's top end with an elastic band. Bring the unlike pole of another magnet near. How far can it pull the ruler? Stronger magnets pull it farther.

MAGNETS AND THEIR USES

MAGNETS are more complicated than they might seem at first. There are different shapes and sizes with different strengths of magnetic fields. They have north and south poles that attract or repel. These features make magnets very useful. They are found in hundreds of tools, toys, machines and gadgets, from small magnets on cupboard door catches to giant magnets in the motors of electric trains. The magnets used in these gadgets are permanent magnets. Their magnetism lasts for years and can be used in many different ways. How many things containing magnets do you notice around your home?

Each of the brightly coloured plastic letters and numbers has a small magnet inside it. This sticks to the white board because the board is a thin sheet of material containing iron.

Magnetic disk
Out of its protective case, a computer disk looks like a dark plastic circle. It has a thin iron-based coating that can hold millions of bits of information as microscopic patches of magnetism.

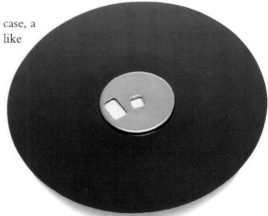

Magnetic motor
Almost anything with an electric motor has a magnet, because magnetism is how the motor turns around. This includes electric drills, screwdrivers and similar tools, whether they use batteries for electricity, or the mains electricity supply from a wall socket.

Magnetic tin-opener

Some tin-openers have a magnet in an arm that touches the top of the tin. As it is opened, the lid stays attached to the magnet, so you are less likely to cut yourself on its sharp edge. These food containers are made of steel coated with tin.

Magnetic holder

A magnet can attract and hold small iron or steel objects such as paper-clips, drawing pins, sewing needles and dressmaking pins. This container is designed to hold paper-clips or pins and has a magnetic lid to attract them. If you accidentally drop them all over the floor, sweeping this magnetic lid over them helps pick them up again.

FACT BOX

• Magnets are often used in recycling. They are used to separate out cans that contain iron or iron alloys from those that are made of aluminium.

• Fridge doors have a magnetic strip around their edge. This sticks to the fridge when the door is closed, keeping it firmly in place and stopping warm air from getting inside and spoiling the food.

• Magnets prevent motor engines from becoming damaged. As oil passes through the mechanism, it picks up tiny bits of steel that are being worn away. Special magnetic plugs pick up these filings and wash them into the sump, a container for the oil.

Magnetic screwdriver

Some screwdrivers are magnetic too. The steel shaft is a long bar magnet. This helps small steel screws to stick to the end as you use them. You can also use the screwdriver to lift small iron-containing objects out of odd places.

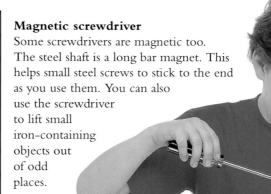

MAGNETIC FISHING

Magnets on lines or ropes can be used to fish iron-containing things out of awkward places. Salvage crews, for example, use huge magnets to recover pieces of wrecked ships and other equipment from the sea bed. The magnets are used where the locations are dangerous, or in murky water, mud and dark holes, where the items cannot be seen or reached without difficulty. The magnetic fishing game belows demonstrates how magnets are used in such a way.

This is a powerful example of how much strength a magnet can have. This magnet was displayed at a technological exhibition in London in the 1920s.

M A T E R I A L S

You will need: different coloured plastic bags, marker pen, scissors, steel paper-clips, magnets, string, wooden rods, sticky tape, deep plate or shallow bowl, watering can, water.

Fishing to win

1 Draw some fish shapes on to the coloured plastic with the marker pen. Cut out the shapes carefully with the scissors.

2 Decorate the fish with the marker pen. Draw scales on one side and write different numbers on the other side of each fish.

3 Attach a steel paper-clip to each fish. Make sure it is firmly attached. This will allow you to catch the fish with a magnetic rod.

4 Tie a magnet to one end of a piece of coloured string. If you tie the string around the middle of the magnet, it will be quite secure.

5 Tape the string attached to the magnet to the end of a wooden rod with sticky tape. Make sure it is stuck on securely.

6 Put in your fish scale-side up and fill the plastic bowl or plate with water. You are now ready to start the fishing game.

Warning
Keep plastic bags away from small children as these bags can be very dangerous.

Playing the fishing game
Each player should dangle their fishing rod over the plastic bowl. When one of the players says 'Go' lower your fishing rods into the water to catch the fish. The steel paper-clips on the fish will be attracted to the magnets on the end of the rods. Carefully lift your fish out of the pond. Each player can make their own pile of fish. When there are no fish left in the bowl, each player counts up the points on the back of their fish and the highest score wins.

THE BIGGEST MAGNET

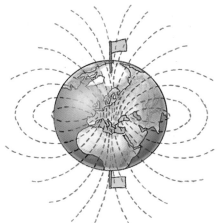

W HAT is the biggest magnet in the world? You are
sitting or standing on it right now! It is the world.
Planet Earth is like a giant magnet. Its magnetism is weak,
however. We do not usually notice it except when
magnetic compasses are used to detect it and find north
and south. Then the Earth's magnetism is very useful. The
force that pulls things down to the centre of the Earth and
makes them fall to the ground is not magnetism. It is called
gravity. It affects everything, whether it is magnetic or not.

*Think of the Earth as a giant
magnet spinning through Space.
Its lines of magnetic force extend
out into Space.*

The iron core
How does the Earth make
its magnetism? Scientists
believe it may be due to
electric currents flowing in
the core, the huge and solid
centre of the planet. The
core is mostly made of iron
and nickel, which is under
enormous pressure and at
a very high temperature.
The flowing movements
may make the magnetism,
like a huge bar magnet inside
the world.

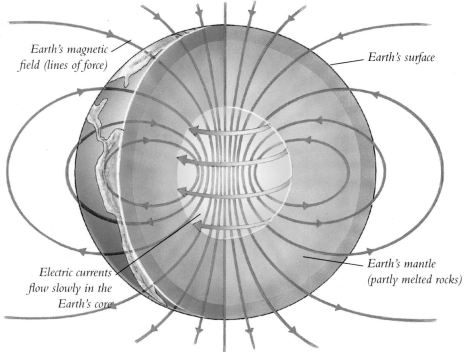

*Earth's magnetic
field (lines of force)*

Earth's surface

*Electric currents
flow slowly in the
Earth's core*

*Earth's mantle
(partly melted rocks)*

Warm winds and sunshine

Winds that blow up from the south to Europe bring warm, dry air from the Sahara Desert region of North Africa. Sometimes we describe a wind by the direction that it is blowing from. The name of this direction comes from the names of the Earth's magnetic poles. Easterly and westerly winds come from directions at right angles to the North and South Poles.

Magnetic storms

Some types of storms and thunderclouds have immense amounts of magnetism and electricity in them, much stronger than Earth's normal magnetic field. They are called magnetic storms. They can affect radio and television sets by disturbing the radio waves that these pick up.

Cold winds and snow

The north wind doth blow, and we shall have snow, goes the rhyme. Winds blowing from a certain direction usually bring different kinds of weather. In Europe and North America, winds from the north bring cold air, frost and snow down from the North Pole and Arctic region.

HOW A COMPASS WORKS

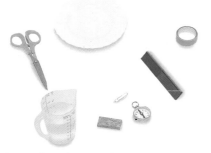

You will need: paper-clip, strong magnet, sticky tape, scissors, piece of cork tile, deep plate or shallow bowl, water, ready-made compass.

IF you were a sailor or an explorer, setting off on an exciting journey into unknown lands, one of the most important things you could have would be a compass. The compass needle is a simple magnet. It is long and thin so that it can spin freely around on a pivot. This simple instrument has saved countless lives, from people lost in the jungle or desert to sailors cast adrift at sea. It has many useful features, even compared to modern devices such as electronic satellite navigation, equipment that uses the GPS (Global Positioning System). The magnetic compass is small, simple to use and reliable. It needs no batteries or fuel. Used correctly, it is very accurate. When looked after properly, a good compass should last a lifetime.

Making a simple compass

1 Straighten out a paper-clip. Stroke it about 50 times with one pole of a magnet. Always stroke in the same direction. Tape the paper-clip, which is now a magnet, to the cork. Float it in a bowl of water.

2 The paper-clip magnet should point north and south. Its north pole is attracted to the Earth's North Pole. Check it and compare it with a ready-made compass. Is your paper-clip magnet accurate?

3 If you bring a strong magnet near to a compass, its magnetic field overpowers the Earth's magnetic field. It attracts the compass, which now lines up with the nearby magnet.

Using a compass

To use a ready-made compass, hold it level and steady so that the needle can spin freely. Let it settle and note where it points. Do this several times to check that the needle does not stick on the base or on its pivot. Carefully turn the base so the N, or north, lines up with the needle. This usually has a spot of paint or an N to indicate its north-seeking end. Compare your home-made paper-clip compass with the ready-made one. Remember that a compass needle or pointer is a magnet. What happens if you put your home-made paper-clip compass very near the ready-made compass needle? Do they swing around to point at each other? They may do, since their unlike poles will attract each other while the like ones repel.

Making a loop compass

1 Straighten out a paper-clip. Magnetize it by stroking it with the strong magnet. Cut a disc of card and bend the wire into a large loop and insert it into the card.

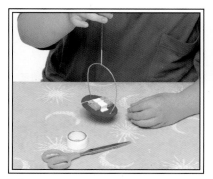

2 Tape the paper-clip to the piece of cork tile and to the card disc. Tie the thread to the top of the wire loop. Let it hang and twirl around freely. It is now ready to test.

3 Does the paper-clip magnet work as a compass needle and point north and south? Check it with the ready-made compass and what do you find?

THE MAGNETIC POLES

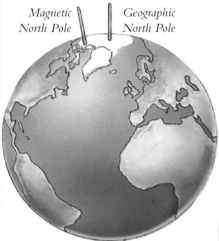

The Geographic Poles indicate the Earth's axis, the imaginary line around which it spins in Space. The Magnetic Poles show where the Earth's magnetism is concentrated.

THE Earth is like a giant magnet – so it must have two poles. We call them the Magnetic north pole and the Magnetic south pole. However, there is another pair of poles – the Geographic North Pole and the Geographic South Pole. They are in different places from their matching Magnetic Poles. The Magnetic Poles are where a compass points to. The Geographic Poles mark the line or axis that the Earth spins around. The areas around the poles are called the polar regions. They are at the top and bottom of the world, where the Sun's warmth is very weak, so they are very cold!

A polar gap

Due to the way the Earth's magnetic field is generated, the direction of the Earth's magnetism is at a slight angle to the Earth's axis. The Magnetic north pole is among the islands of northern North America, several hundred kilometres from the Geographic North Pole. A compass needle points to the Magnetic north pole.

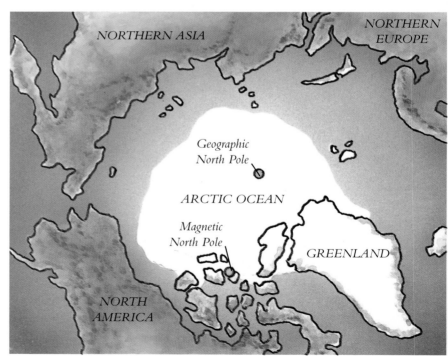

Race to the North Pole

The Geographic North Pole is in the middle of the Arctic Ocean, which is always covered by a layer of ice. The first explorer to walk there across the dangerous, shifting ice-cap was probably American Robert Peary in 1909 *(left)*. However, some experts say that he did not reach the exact Geographic North Pole.

Fossil ferns in the snow

The land near the North Pole is now snow-covered. Millions of years ago it was warm so that ferns and plants flourished.

Race to the South Pole

The Geographic South Pole is on the great southern continent of Antarctica, which is completely covered by thick ice for nearly all of the year. In 1911 two teams of explorers raced to get there. Norwegian Roald Amundsen's group was first and returned safely. British Robert Falcon Scott's *(right)* expedition arrived one month later. On arrival, they found a sympathetic note from Amundsen. Sadly, Scott and his men did not survive the return journey.

MAGNETS IN SPACE

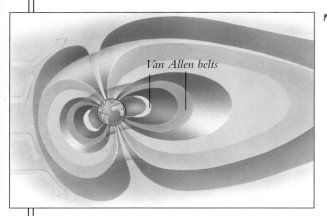

Van Allen belts

The magnetosphere is the region in Space around the Earth where the solar wind from the Sun blows through the Earth's magnetic field. It is like a giant lop-sided doughnut. It has several layers, including the Van Allen belts, named after the scientist who discovered them from satellite information.

THE Earth's magnetism is not just down on the ground, where we detect it with compasses. Like any other magnet, the Earth's magnetic field extends away from it, into the air – and even right out into Space. But the magnetic field is not equal on both sides of the planet, as it is with most ordinary magnets. A stream of energy and particles from the Sun, called the solar wind, blows against the magnetic field and makes it lop-sided. This vast region, where the magnetic field meets the solar wind, is called the magnetosphere. It extends for thousands of kilometres into Space, especially on the night side of the Earth, away from the Sun.

Magnetism in deep Space
Powerful telescopes and satellite equipment show that there is magnetism deep in Space. It is usually concentrated around incredibly vast objects like galaxies and quasars. The magnetism is powerful, billions of times stronger than any magnets made on Earth.

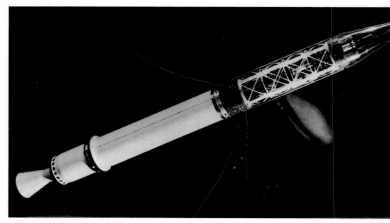

Finding the field
In 1958 one of the first satellites, *Explorer 1*, detected magnetic layers around the Earth. In the early 1960s, *Explorer 12* proved that the magnetosphere existed. Its scientific instruments detected the magnetism and energy far into Space, and how these varied.

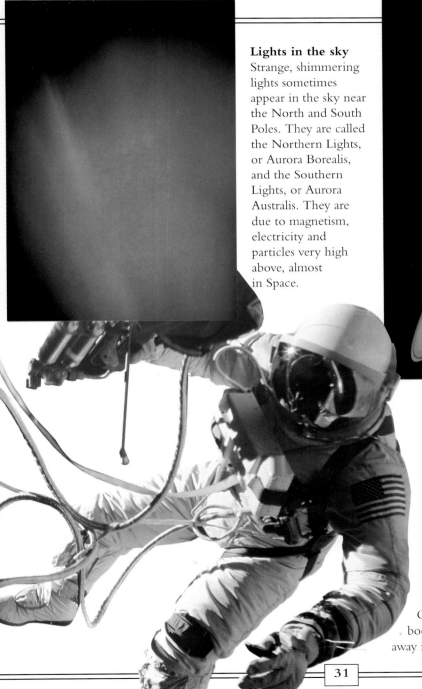

Lights in the sky

Strange, shimmering lights sometimes appear in the sky near the North and South Poles. They are called the Northern Lights, or Aurora Borealis, and the Southern Lights, or Aurora Australis. They are due to magnetism, electricity and particles very high above, almost in Space.

The planets

Several planets in our Solar System are magnetic. They have their own magnetic fields and magnetospheres like Earth. They include the small planet nearest the Sun, called Mercury, and the giant planets much farther away, Jupiter and Saturn *(above)*.

Space walk

Magnetism in Space is sometimes very useful. Astronauts use magnetic holders to stop things drifting around in the weightless conditions inside the spacecraft. Outside, during a Space walk, magnetic boots, gloves and holders stop things drifting away into Space. That includes the astronaut!

MAGNETS AND MAPS

L OOK at a map – which way up does it go? Maps are made according to the Earth's magnetism and the magnetic compass. They have north at the top, in the same way that the North Pole is at the top of the world. We are used to looking at maps and using them with north at the top, pointing straight up or away from us. Look on a local map to find a diagram of the compass points, an arrow or N that indicates north. Then, using a compass, turn the map so that its north faces the same way as the compass north. Now the map is lined up accurately in relation to the landscape. If you are on a hilltop with wide views, you can see how the map is a tiny version of the countryside all around.

Maps are important because they enable us to know where we are going. Without magnets we would not know how to use a map or find our way around.

Which way up?
We are so familiar with maps having north at the top, that they look odd when they are turned around. Can you recognize this country *(left)* when it is turned upside down? Can you find it on the globe *(right)?*

The compass maze
Can you find your way through
this maze? When you have made
it to the other side, try recording
your route with compass points.
At the beginning of the journey,
you head east, turn north and
then go east again. Can you
complete these instructions for
the entire journey?

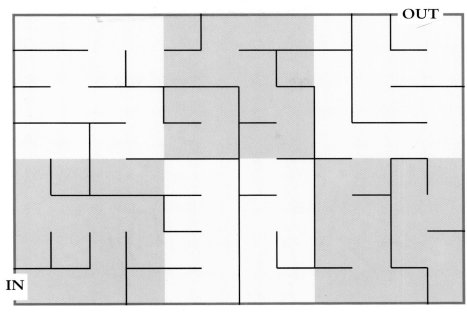

OUT

IN

N
W E
S

Drawing a maze

M A T E R I A L S

*You will need: card,
coloured pens, compass.*

1 Draw your own maze. Make it
colourful and fun. Put in some
dead ends and false turns. Make sure
that one route leads all the way
through from one end of the maze
to another, even though it may be
very twisty!

2 Now record your course
through the maze, using compass
points for the directions. You can
limit the information to north,
south, east and west, or include
more detailed directions such as
north-east and south-west.

MAGNETIC SENSE

Magnetism is probably an important guide to the Arctic tern on its migratory route. It flies to the far north of the Arctic for the summer. To avoid the long northern winter, it flies around the world to the far south, even to Antarctica.

WE cannot detect magnets or magnetic fields with our own bodies. However, various animals seem to sense magnetism. They may detect the Earth's magnetic field and use it to help them navigate, or find their way, on very long journeys called migrations. Like human sailors or explorers using a magnetic compass, these animals seem to have a built-in body compass. Many kinds of animals migrate. They include swallows, geese and various other birds, fish like salmon and large mammals such as whales, seals and caribou. Scientists have not yet discovered where this natural compass might be in the animal's body, or exactly how it works.

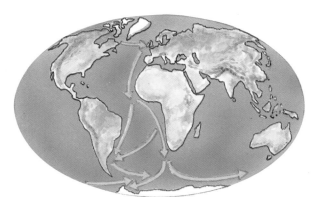

Migration route
The tern's migration follows the Earth's lines of magnetic force. It flies from north to south and then returns later in the year, from south to north. Birds probably use several clues to navigate, such as rivers, mountains, coastlines, the positions of the Sun, Moon and stars, and magnetism.

Whales at sea
Many great whales and other types of sea mammal go on long, annual journeys. They usually start from their winter area of warm tropical sea and move to their summer area of polar seas, where food is plentiful. Like other migrating sea animals, they probably use several clues to find their way, such as coastlines, undersea mountains or cliffs, sea currents, the Earth's gravity and magnetism.

Turtle travellers

Sea turtles also wander the world's oceans, yet they return to the beach where they hatched from eggs, to lay their own eggs.

To the north

The usual reason for migration is to travel to a place where conditions are good for a limited time. In the short Arctic summer, plants grow quickly and plentifully. Birds such as geese fly there to breed. Insects such as the monarch butterfly also go on long annual migrations.

Where is the body compass?

Experiments with pigeons show that they probably use magnetism to navigate. When scientists strapped a small but strong magnet to a pigeon's head, this interfered with the Earth's magnetic field – and the pigeon lost its way! A bird's own body compass may be somewhere inside its head, near or inside the brain.

ELECTRIC MAGNETS

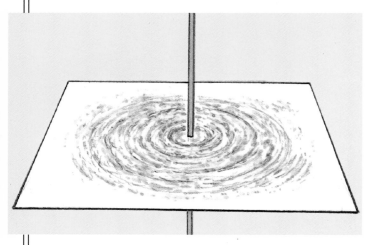

The magnetic field around a wire with electricity flowing through it can be made stronger by wrapping the wire in a coil around an iron bar. The iron bar then works like a bar magnet – but only while electricity flows. This simple device, the electromagnet, is a magnet that you can switch on and off. Electromagnets are found in their millions in all kinds of machinery.

THE ordinary bar and horseshoe magnets are permanent magnets. They have what scientists call spontaneous permanent magnetism. Their magnetism needs no outside force or energy. But there is another way of making magnetism – by electricity. When electricity flows through a wire or another similar conductor (electricity-carrier), it produces a magnetic field around the wire. This is called electromagnetism or EM. In fact, magnetism and electricity are very closely linked. Each can be used to make the other. EM is used in thousands of kinds of tools, machines and devices that are vital in our modern world.

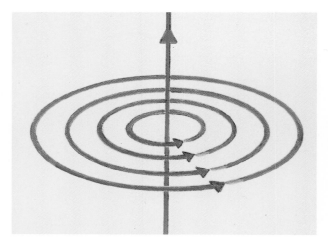

Seeing electromagnetism
If iron filings are sprinkled on to a card that has an electricity-carrying wire through it, the filings are affected by the magnetic field. They arrange themselves in circles to show the lines of magnetic force, as they do with an ordinary magnet.

Creating a magnetic field
As electricity flows through a wire, a magnetic field is created around it. The magnetic lines of force flow in circles around the wire. This is called an electromagnetic field. As soon as the electricity is switched off, the magnetism stops.

EM in toys

Many toys have electromagnets inside them. This battery-operated car is steered by using two electromagnets at the front. One twists the wheels so the car turns left and the other makes it go to the right. With both of the electromagnets switched off, a spring pulls the wheels so the car goes straight.

FACT BOX

• In Denmark, the scientist Hans Christian Oersted (1777-1851) was the first to discover that an electric current produced magnetism, in 1820. During a talk to students, he noticed that a compass needle was affected by a nearby electricity-carrying wire.

• In France, André Marie Ampère (1775-1836) did many experiments on electricity and magnetism. He invented the idea of twisting wire into a coil, called a solenoid, to make its magnetism stronger.

• In England, Michael Faraday (1791-1867) discovered electromagnetic induction, using magnetism to generate an electic current. This led to many useful inventions, including the electric motor, dynamo and transformer.

• In the USA, Joseph Henry (1797-1878) also discovered electromagnetic induction and how to make an electric motor. He made incredibly powerful electromagnets that lifted weights of over one tonne.

Switch on and off

One of the most useful features of an electromagnet is that you can switch it on and off. Large electromagnets are strong enough to pick up old cars by their steel roofs and drop them into the car-crusher. Many machines and equipment rely on electromagnets for their effectiveness.

MAKING AN ELECTROMAGNET

T HE magnetism of an electromagnet is the same as magnetism from an ordinary magnet. It is just the way of making it that differs. The first practical useful electromagnets were made by British bootmaker and spare-time scientist William Sturgeon in the 1820s to amaze audiences at his science shows. The basic design has hardly changed since. You can make a similar electromagnet and amaze your friends, too!

M A T E R I A L S

You will need: wire-strippers, about two metres of ordinary wire (insulated, plastic-coated, multi-strand copper), large iron nail, bar or rod, 9-volt battery, paper-clips, piece of card, split-pins.

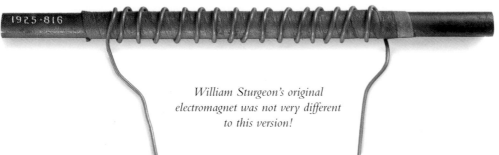

William Sturgeon's original electromagnet was not very different to this version!

Your own electromagnet

1 Using the wire-strippers, carefully remove a few centimetres of plastic insulation from each end of the wire. These bare ends will connect to the battery.

2 Carefully wrap the wire in a tight coil around the iron nail. The insulation around the wire conducts the electricity around the iron nail.

3 Connect the wire's ends to the battery terminals. (It does not matter which is positive or negative.) Test your electromagnet by picking up paper-clips.

Stronger magnets

This electromagnet *(left)* has two sets of coils, one on top of the other, but all made from one length of wire. There are several ways of making an electromagnet stronger and more powerful. One is to put more turns of wire on to the central iron rod or bar. You could try making your own version of this with a longer piece of wire. Wrap one set of turns around the nail. Then make another set of turns to form a second coil on top of the first. Another way is to use more electricity, such as two 9-volt batteries. In this project electricity flows as soon as the wires are joined to the battery. This can quickly make the battery run down or flat. It is better to have a switch, so you can turn the electromagnet on and off easily, as needed.

Warning

NEVER try using electricity from the mains socket on the wall. It is far too dangerous and could kill. Ask an adult for help in this project.

Adding a switch

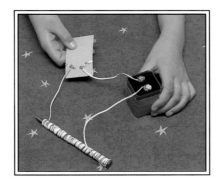

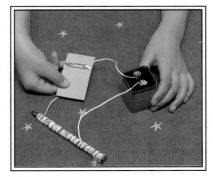

1 Make two equal-sized holes in the piece of card. Push the split-pins into them. Push one of the split-pins through a paper-clip first. Open out the legs of the split-pins. Each leg is now ready to connect to the wire.

2 Connect one end of the electromagnet wire to the split-pin. Connect the other to a battery terminal. Join the remaining split-pin to the other battery terminal with another short piece of wire. Turn the card over.

3 The paper-clip fixed to one split-pin is the switch. Push it away from the other split-pin and notice that no electricity flows. Turn the paper-clip to touch the split-pin. Electricity flows, switching on the electromagnet.

EM MACHINES

Hundreds of machines use the switchable on–off magnetic power of electromagnetism. You can find them around the home, at school, in factories and offices, in the car, the garage, the supermarket – just about everywhere. Some electromagnetic machines use the electricity from batteries. Others need the much more powerful mains electricity from wall sockets.

A metal detector uses electromagnetism to signal if iron-containing substances are nearby. Some detectors can also locate other types of metals. They work by battery power.

Medical scanners

The magnetic resonance imager (MRI) is a type of scanner that can see inside the body. The person is put into a huge electromagnet, which uses a combination of magnetism and radio waves to detect different parts inside the body. A computer processes the results and shows them on a screen.

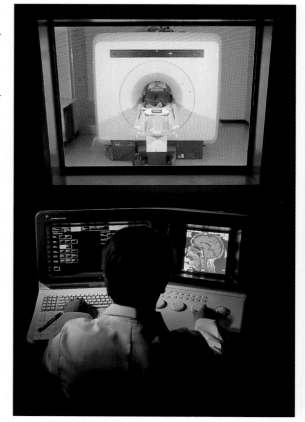

Recycling

At some recycling banks, aluminium drinks cans and steel food cans all go into the same container. At the recycling works, an electromagnet separates them by attracting the steel ones but not the aluminium ones.

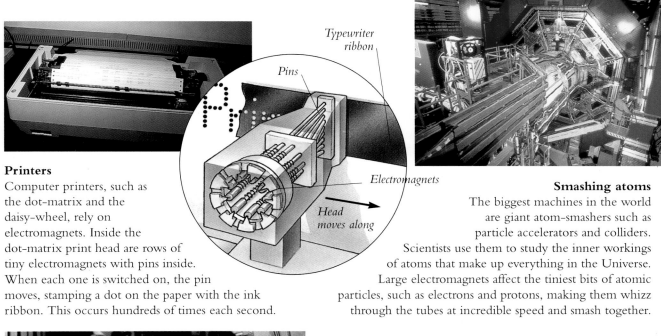

Printers

Computer printers, such as the dot-matrix and the daisy-wheel, rely on electromagnets. Inside the dot-matrix print head are rows of tiny electromagnets with pins inside. When each one is switched on, the pin moves, stamping a dot on the paper with the ink ribbon. This occurs hundreds of times each second.

Typewriter ribbon

Pins

Electromagnets

Head moves along

Smashing atoms

The biggest machines in the world are giant atom-smashers such as particle accelerators and colliders. Scientists use them to study the inner workings of atoms that make up everything in the Universe. Large electromagnets affect the tiniest bits of atomic particles, such as electrons and protons, making them whizz through the tubes at incredible speed and smash together.

Making televisions

These people are putting together televisions in a factory in Japan. Magnets are an important part of the electrical circuits found in the back of a television set.

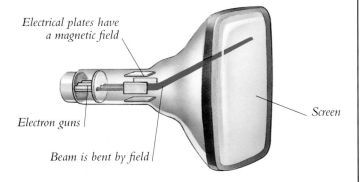

Electrical plates have a magnetic field

Electron guns

Beam is bent by field

Screen

Inside the television

Television sets, computer monitors and similar screens have electromagnet-type devices inside. They are usually shaped like flat plates. They bend the beam that scans across the screen, line by line, to build up the picture. This occurs many times every second.

THE EM OLYMPICS

ELECTROMAGNETS are found in many toys and games. You can use the power of electromagnetism to make your own game, the EM Olympics. Here, a washer represents a discus, a nut a shot-put and a nail a javelin. The electromagnet is used to throw each of them. The secret of success is in the timing. At the exact moment when you switch off the electromagnet, it stops attracting the iron or steel object and releases it.

Throwing the real javelin is one of several Olympic field events. The sport probably began in ancient times with spears.

You will need: sheets of card, scissors, glue, marker pen, decorative stick-on shapes, large iron nail, insulated (plastic-coated) copper wire, wire-strippers, paper-clip, split-pins, battery, sticky tape, washer, small nails, nut.

The EM games

1 Cut a sheet of card into a base about 30–40 cm long and wide. Cut four strips the same length and 8–12 cm deep, for the sides. Glue the sides and base together.

2 Cut out squares of card for the scoreboard and tape them together to make a sheet that will fit neatly into the box. Write scores on them and decorate them.

3 Fit the scoreboard into the box. It is best not to glue it, since you may wish to take it out and alter the scores, or make a new scoreboard as you become an expert at the games.

A cat's entrance
This type of cat flap can be opened only by a cat wearing a special collar with an electromagnet attached to it. A switch is flicked when the cat pushes against the flap.

4   Cut out two more long, wide strips of card. Tape them together at two of their short edges. Glue the other short edges inside the box, on opposite sides. Position this 'arch' at one end of the box.

5   Make an electromagnet from the nail and the wire. Tape it to the arch so that it can hang below by its wires. Connect the free ends of the wire to the battery. Use a paper-clip to make a switch for the battery.

6   Push the nail electromagnet to and fro to test that it swings freely. In turn, put iron or steel objects in the box – use a nail as a javelin, a nut as a shot-put and a washer as a discus. Switch on the nail electromagnet. Push the nail electromagnet to make it swing. As it moves, it should pull the items in the box with it. Turn off the switch and they will be released. Note where they land on the scoreboard.

MAGNETISM IN MOTORS

THE electric motor changes electricity, using magnetism, into a turning or spinning force that has thousands of uses. There is also a machine that does the opposite. It changes a turning force, using magnetism, into electricity. This is called a dynamo or generator. It is this machine that makes electricity in power stations. Electromagnetic machines such as the motor and generator are essential to modern life.

This simple piece of equipment is a metal ring wrapped in coils of wire. Michael Faraday and other scientists used it to study electricity and magnetism. With its help they invented machines such as the electric motor, dynamo and transformer.

Electric motor

An electric motor has a wire coil positioned between permanent magnets. Electricity flows and makes the coil an electromagnet. But the electricity's direction means the coil's magnetic poles are the same as the nearest poles of the permanent magnet – and like poles repel. So the coil spins around. However, the two-part turning contact called the commutator spins with the coil and reverses the electricity's direction. This reverses the coil's electromagnetic poles, while the permanent magnet's poles stay the same. Again, like poles repel, so the coil twirls a bit more. The commutator reverses the electricity again and a cycle is set up.

Commutator

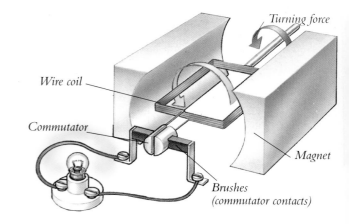

Turning force

Wire coil

Commutator

Magnet

Brushes (commutator contacts)

Electric dynamo

A dynamo has almost exactly the same parts as an electric motor. But the coil is turned around by an outside force, such as a petrol engine, a steam turbine, or even a handle driven by hand! As the coil turns around in the magnetic field of the permanent magnet, electricity is generated in its wires. This is called electromagnetic induction.

- In 1821 Michael Faraday invented a simple device that used electricity and magnetism to make a wire twirl around a magnet.

- The first practical electric motor was described by Joseph Henry in 1831.

- By the late 1830s, many designs of electric motors were being tested.

- The first generators were made in 1832, by Hippolyte Pixii. They made electricity from movement. Previously, people could only make electricity from chemicals, in electric cells or batteries.

Big motors

Electric trains, like this subway train, have huge electric motors to turn the wheels around. Each pair of wheels on their axle has their own motor.

Small motors

A tiny electric motor, as small as a thimble, makes the tape move along in a personal stereo cassette-player. Similar motors make a compact disc spin around in a CD player.

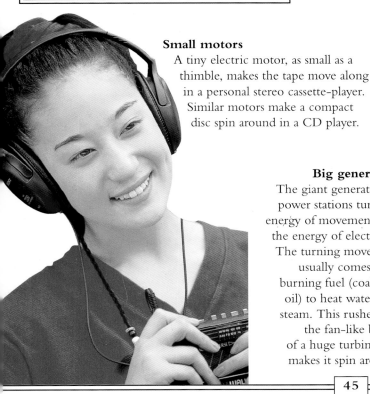

Big generators

The giant generators in power stations turn the energy of movement into the energy of electricity. The turning movement usually comes from burning fuel (coal, gas, oil) to heat water into steam. This rushes past the fan-like blades of a huge turbine and makes it spin around.

MOTORIZED MACHINES

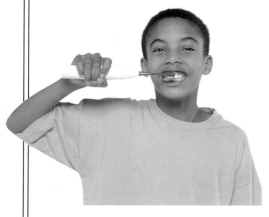

How many electric motors are near you, right now? There are probably more than you realize. In a house packed with gadgets, there are motors in the washing machine, spin dryer, tumble-dryer, dishwasher, microwave oven turntable, vacuum cleaner, electric food mixer, electric tin-opener, central heating pump, cooling fan, CD player, tape-player, computer CD and disk drives, toys such as cars and robots - the list is very long! Next time you are in a classroom, workshop, garage, office, factory or similar place, see how many electric motors you can spot.

Brushing
An electric toothbrush has a small motor inside it, in the handle near the batteries. It turns an arm mechanism that makes the brush head vibrate or move to and fro very rapidly.

Blowing
An electric motor in a hair-dryer turns a fan that blows cool air through the fan's heater to make it warm. Warm air blows out of the nozzle. A switch alters the amount of electricity fed to the fan motor to change the amount of blown air.

Rolling
Most toy cars and trucks work by electric motors. The motor spins around and turns the wheels, usually through a set of gears to slow down the spinning speed. Bigger vehicles also use electric motors including golf buggies, milk floats, taxis and buses.

Drilling

The electric drill has a strong motor that twists the drill bit around so it can bore holes in wood, brick and even concrete. Similar motors are used in many other electric tools and appliances, such as electric saws, screwdrivers, sanders, mowers, strimmers and hedge-trimmers.

Starting

Without the large and powerful electric motor that turns the engine to start a car, you would have to start it by turning a handle! A luxury car has dozens of other electric motors to work the fuel pump, windscreen wipers, windscreen washers, electric windows, electric seat adjusters and many other things. The list is almost endless.

SOUND TO MAGNETISM

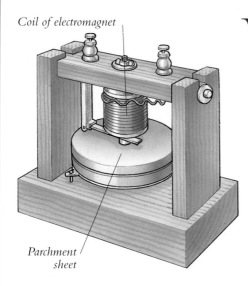

Coil of electromagnet

Parchment sheet

In the first telephones, sound waves from the voice hit a large piece of parchment paper that was stretched tight like a drum skin. This made it vibrate. The paper was attached to a magnet, which also vibrated – within a wire coil. The magnet moving near the coil created electricity in the coil.

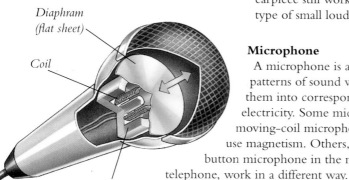

Diaphram (flat sheet)

Coil

Magnet

WE have seen that movement can be converted into electricity, using magnetism. When a wire or similar object moves within the magnetic field of a magnet, the wire passes or cuts the lines of magnetic force. As it does so, electricity is generated in the wire. The process is called electromagnetic induction. It is used in many machines and devices, such as dynamos or generators and electric guitars. Sound is a type of movement. It is the to-and-fro vibrations in air. Sound can be converted into electricity too, using magnetism. In the 1870s, Alexander Graham Bell invented the first telephone using a combination of sound, magnetism and electricity.

On the line
The modern telephone has a mouthpiece that picks up the sounds of your voice and changes them to electricity. It works in a different way to the mouthpiece of the early telephone. However, the earpiece still works as a type of small loudspeaker.

Microphone
A microphone is a device that detects patterns of sound waves and turns them into corresponding patterns of electricity. Some microphones, like the moving-coil microphone shown here, use magnetism. Others, like the carbon button microphone in the mouthpiece of a telephone, work in a different way.

Early microphones
The early microphones used by radio stations were very large and cumbersome. The one shown on the left dates back to 1924.

Modern microphones
Microphones are easier and smaller to move around. They also pick up sounds more accurately.

Two-way radio
Walkie-talkies *(right)*, two-way radios and mobile phones all use microphones and loudspeakers. These types of microphones are designed to be simple, tough and reliable. They pick up the sounds of the human voice. Other microphones are designed to pick up the sounds of musical instruments such as a piano or violin.

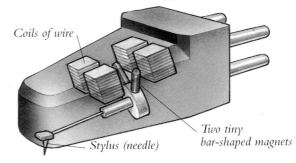

Coils of wire

Two tiny bar-shaped magnets

Stylus (needle)

Vinyl pick-up
Vinyl records are usually played using a moving-coil magnetic pick-up. This has a tiny pointed stylus needle that vibrates as it follows the wavy groove on the record. The vibrations shake two tiny bar-shaped magnets inside. Their magnetic fields affect small coils of wire nearby, creating patterns of electricity that follow the patterns of vibrations.

MAGNETS AS STORAGE SPACE

Patches of magnetism on tape are codes for sounds

RECORDED music and sound are part of our daily life. We play cassette tapes, video tapes and perhaps reel-to-reel tapes. We tune into music, speech and other sounds on the radio and television that have been recorded earlier on tape. Without magnetism, these tapes would not be possible. The sounds are recorded, or stored, as tiny patches of magnetism, which are far too small to see. The patches stay in the tape for many years without fading. The process of recording sounds on magnetic tape began in the 1930s. Today it is used throughout the media business. A magnetic tape has several layers. The base is strong flexible plastic. The magnetic layer has tiny particles of iron-containing substances such as iron oxide, often mixed with other metals such as chrome, to improve the quality.

Magnetic tape stores sounds as micro-dots of magnetism. In fact, the tape stores any kind of information or data in this way, in the form of codes, including sounds, computer programs and files, text and pictures.

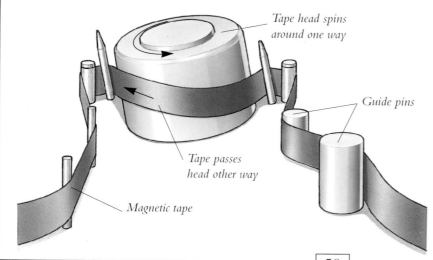

Tape head spins around one way

Guide pins

Tape passes head other way

Magnetic tape

Tape head
In some types of tape recorders, the record and playback heads are the same device. The head spins around one way as the magnetic tape moves past it the other way. Video tape and digital audio tape (DAT) also use these types of rotating heads.

- The first magnetic sound-recorder was invented in 1898, by Valdemar Poulsen. It was not a tape recorder, but a wire recorder, using a long piece of steel wire.

- The first tape recorders used metal tape. They were invented in 1928.

- In the 1930s, the tape was changed from metal to plastic with a very thin iron coating. This is the type of tape used today.

- Sounds can also be recorded or stored non-magnetically – as a wavy groove in a vinyl record disc, or as tiny lumps and pits read by laser light, on a CD.

The cassette

In the 1960s Philips introduced a mini reel of magnetic tape inside its own small case, or case-ette. This was much more convenient than a large reel of tape that might unroll and spill everywhere. At first, its recording quality was not good, but it has improved.

Recording studio

The sound engineer sits in the control room at a huge desk called the mixing console. The performers are in a separate sound-proofed studio room, visible through the window. In the foreground, a reel-to-reel tape recorder stores the sounds as magnetism.

Reel-to-reel

Inside this broadcast van there are high quality tape recorders that use long pieces of wide magnetic tape wound on to reels. The patches of magnetism are put on to the blank tape by the record head. They are picked up by the playback head, or they can be wiped off to make the tape blank again by the erase head. These heads are all types of electromagnets.

MAGNETISM AND SOUND

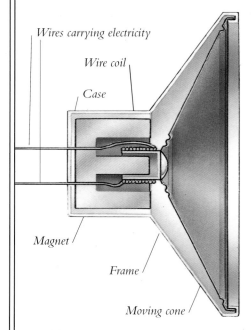

Wires carrying electricity

Wire coil

Case

Magnet

Frame

Moving cone

THERE would not be much point in recording sounds, pictures and other information on magnetic tape unless you could replay the tape and get back what you started with. Most tape machines can both record and play back, although personal stereo cassette-players usually only play back. The playback head is a type of electromagnet that detects the patterns of magnetism on the tape and turns them into patterns of electricity. For sound, the main device that turns these electrical signals back into sounds is the loudspeaker. These types of devices are also found in headphones and in the earpiece of a telephone.

Diaphragm (thin sheet)

Magnets

Diaphragm (thin sheet)

Head band

Case

Wire coil

Samarium-cobalt magnet

Wires

Spongy earpiece

Inside a loudspeaker

Patterns of varying electrical signals are transferred to the loudspeaker along the connecting wire or speaker lead. They go through the wire coil, which is attached to the large card or plastic speaker cone. The signals make the coil into an electromagnet that varies in strength. This magnetic field is itself inside the field of a strong permanent magnet. The two fields interact, with like poles repelling in the usual way. This makes the coil move or vibrate to and fro, which makes the loudspeaker cone vibrate too. This, in turn, sends out sound waves.

Telephone earpiece

The earpiece *(above)* receives varying patterns of electrical signals from the mouthpiece of the telephone held by the person at the other end of the line. The earpiece works like a simple loudspeaker to recreate the sounds of the other person's voice.

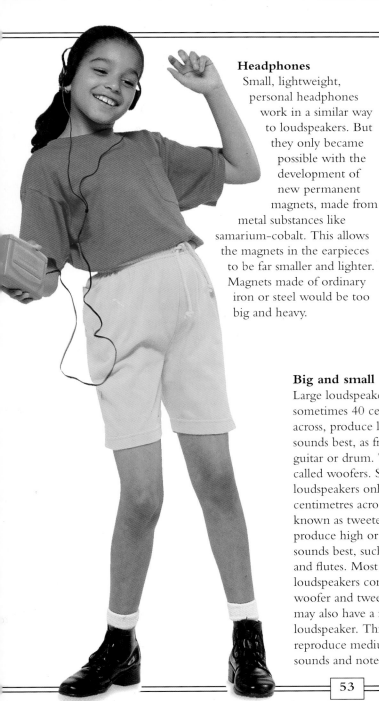

Headphones

Small, lightweight, personal headphones work in a similar way to loudspeakers. But they only became possible with the development of new permanent magnets, made from metal substances like samarium-cobalt. This allows the magnets in the earpieces to be far smaller and lighter. Magnets made of ordinary iron or steel would be too big and heavy.

Big and small

Large loudspeakers, sometimes 40 centimetres across, produce low or deep sounds best, as from a bass guitar or drum. They are called woofers. Small loudspeakers only a few centimetres across are known as tweeters. They produce high or shrill sounds best, such as cymbals and flutes. Most hi-fi loudspeakers contain both a woofer and tweeter. They may also have a mid-range loudspeaker. This helps to reproduce medium-pitched sounds and notes clearly.

MAGNETIC MUSIC

WITHOUT magnetism, we would not have the sound of the electric guitar, and rock music would be very different! An acoustic guitar's sound comes from its vibrating strings, which are made louder by the guitar's hollow body. When you play an electric guitar, it actually sounds very quiet and tinny. An electric guitar uses electromagnetism to make small electrical signals. The guitar is plugged into an amplifier and the signals are fed into it. The amplifier makes these signals stronger and in turn sends them to a loudspeaker (another electromagnetic device) which makes the electrical signals into actual sounds.

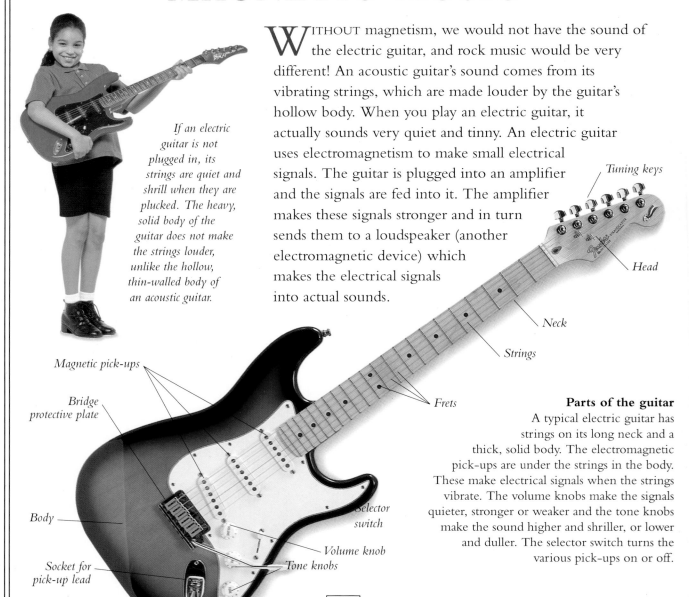

If an electric guitar is not plugged in, its strings are quiet and shrill when they are plucked. The heavy, solid body of the guitar does not make the strings louder, unlike the hollow, thin-walled body of an acoustic guitar.

Tuning keys

Head

Neck

Strings

Frets

Magnetic pick-ups

Bridge protective plate

Body

Socket for pick-up lead

Selector switch

Volume knob

Tone knobs

Parts of the guitar
A typical electric guitar has strings on its long neck and a thick, solid body. The electromagnetic pick-ups are under the strings in the body. These make electrical signals when the strings vibrate. The volume knobs make the signals quieter, stronger or weaker and the tone knobs make the sound higher and shriller, or lower and duller. The selector switch turns the various pick-ups on or off.

54

The pick-up

An electric guitar's pick-up has a plastic cover. Underneath are six small bar-shaped, permanent magnets called pole pieces, with a coil of wire wrapped around them. In many guitars this coil has more than 6,000 turns!

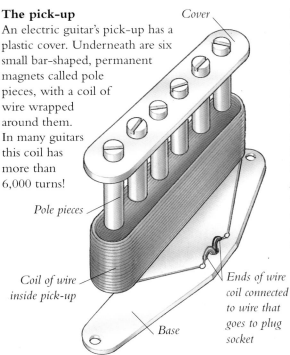

Cover

Pole pieces

Coil of wire inside pick-up

Base

Ends of wire coil connected to wire that goes to plug socket

How the pick-up works

The permanent magnets create a magnetic field around the pick-up. When the metal guitar string is plucked, it vibrates in this field and disturbs it. The variations in magnetism create electrical signals in the wire coil by the process of electromagnetic induction.

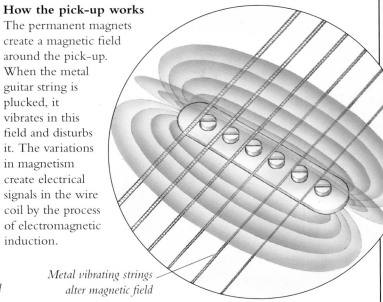

Metal vibrating strings alter magnetic field

Electric piano

Some electric pianos work in the same way as an electric guitar. When you press a key, this plucks a small strip of metal called a reed, making it ping and vibrate. The reed is next to a small magnet wrapped in a wire coil. It creates electrical signals in the same way as the guitar pick-up above. There are also magnets and electromagnets inside modern electronic synthesizers, keyboards and organs.

FACT BOX

• The first guitars with electromagnetic pick-ups were made in the 1930s. One of the earliest was the 1931 *Frying Pan*, shaped like a banjo. It had a pick-up consisting of two horseshoe magnets around a coil of wire.

• The first mass-produced electric guitars were made in 1932 by a company set up by Adolph Rickenbacker.

• The Gibson company started making their designs of electric guitars in about 1935, but these had hollow bodies.

• In 1950 the Fender company launched the *Broadcaster* – the first electric guitar with a solid body, bolt-on neck and two pick-ups. The rock guitar was born!

MAGNETS AND COMPUTERS

This type of computer disk is enclosed in a protective plastic case. Take an old, unwanted disk and slide the silvery metal shutter sideways so that you see the dark, shiny disk inside. It has a layer of iron-containing substance to retain the codes of magnetic patches, as in magnetic recording tape.

SWITCH on a typical desktop PC (Personal Computer) and immediately magnetism goes into action. The MD (magnetic disk) and CD (compact disc) spin around in their disk drives, which use magnetism in their electric motors. Programs and other data are stored on the magnetic disk as microscopic patterns of magnetism, like magnetic recording tape. A type of electromagnet called the read-write head reads, or receives, the information from the magnetic disk so that the computer can start working. Electromagnets in the monitor screen make the beam scan across it line by line to form pictures. If the computer has a cooling fan, this too has an electric motor that works by magnetism.

Push, click
The magnetic disk slots into the computer. The hub of the disk is designed to fit over the drive of a stepper motor. This is a special type of electric motor. It is distinctive because it can spin around very fast, and yet is able to stop with amazing accuracy.

Compact disc
A compact disc has patterns of microscopic bumps. Like the magnetic patches on a magnetic disk, they contain information in coded form. The CD itself does not use magnetism – it is read by a laser beam. It spins around using electromagnetism, in an electric motor (*right*). The surface of a compact disc has millions of tiny bumps. A laser beam shines at these. It reflects from the patches between the bumps, but not from the bumps. The pattern of reflections is picked up by the detector.

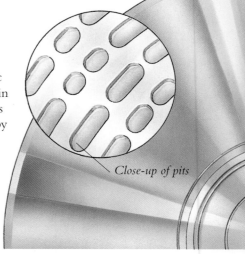

Close-up of pits

Pits and bumps on lower surface of CD

Reading a CD

The CD drive uses a laser beam that shines at the CD's lower surface. It is reflected by the pattern of microscopic pits as the disc spins around driven by an electric motor. The detector picks up the on-off patterns of reflections and converts them into electrical signals for the computer.

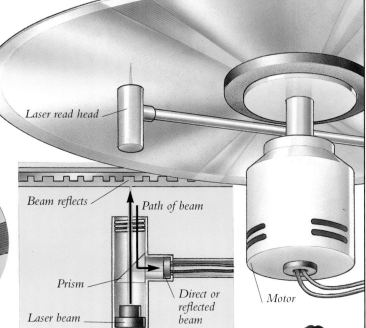

Laser read head

Motor

Read–write head

Computer tape is read by an electromagnetic device similar to the record-playback head on a tape recorder. This reads from the tape by detecting patterns of magnetism, turning them into electrical signals for the computer. It writes on to the tape by recording new magnetic patches on it. A magnetic disk read–write head works in a similar way.

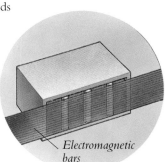

Electromagnetic bars

Beam reflects

Path of beam

Prism

Direct or reflected beam

Laser beam

Computer room

The computer departments of big companies use massive amounts of computer power and need to record vast amounts of information. This is usually done on large reels of magnetic tape or on magnetic disks. These are called storage media.

More on less

The amount of information that can be stored on magnetic disks increases every year. The words and pictures in a whole pile of books can fit on to one small disk. You can only read the disk with an expensive computer. You can read a book with just your eyes!

MAGNETIC *FORMULA 1*

Real Grand Prix cars can travel 300 kilometres per hour, a little faster than a table-top version! They do not use magnetism in their motors as their engines run on petrol-based fuel.

A FORMULA 1 Grand Prix car race is one of the most spectacular events in sport. Racing requires skill and determination. You can make your own table-top version and race your friends, using a few bits of card, other objects and some magnets. Remember your version is special because it uses magnetism. Small, flat bar or ring magnets are best. The trick is to stay on the track and speed along, but not so fast that the magnet loses your car! If that happens, you are out of the race and the game is definitely over. Good luck!

Magnetic racing

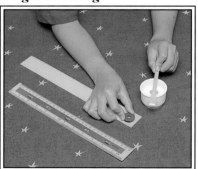

1 Glue a magnet to the end of each ruler. Use 45-centimetre rulers if you can, or similar sized strips of wood.

2 Draw the shapes of racing cars on the coloured card. You can make the wheels a different colour and perhaps add stripes, too.

3 Carefully cut out the car shapes with scissors. Decorate them with stick-on shapes to make up your own racing team.

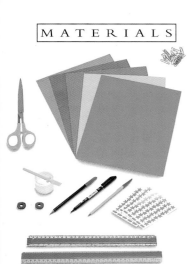

You will need: small ring or bar magnets, glue, two long rulers or strips of wood, sheets of coloured card, pens, scissors, stick-on stars or similar shapes, paper-clips, large sheet of stiff card.

4 Glue a steel paper-clip to the underside of each car. Let the glue dry thoroughly while you make the racing track from card.

5 Draw a circuit on the card to make the track. Put the whole track on two books so that it is raised all around the edge. This lets you get the ruler and magnet underneath. Place your racing cars on the start line. Push the ruler underneath so that the magnet faces upwards and attracts the paper-clip on the base of your car. Move the ruler slowly so that the magnet drags the paper-clip and car along. Practise driving like this for a while. Overtaking is tricky, since you have to manoeuvre your ruler past your opponent's ruler. Good luck!

MAGNETS OF THE FUTURE

THE science of magnets and magnetism never stands still. Every day people are doing tests and experiments to make more powerful magnets, with better combinations of metals and improved designs of wire coils. Progress in electromagnets helps to design better medical scanners, atom-smashers and electric motors for all kinds of equipment and machinery. In the future, magnets will become even more important in our world.

The latest electromagnets (left) use special combinations of metals and incredible amounts of electricity. They are super-cooled to allow the electricity to flow around the wire coil more easily. They produce magnetic fields that last only a fraction of a second. Yet they have the same energy as an exploding bomb.

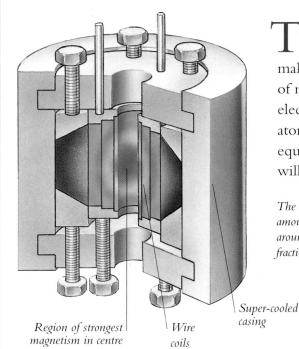

Region of strongest magnetism in centre

Wire coils

Super-cooled casing

Plasma power

A new design for a power station involves heating substances to incredibly high temperatures so that they are not solid, or liquid, or gas, but a different form of matter – plasma. The plasma is so hot and dangerous that it cannot touch the sides of the reactor. It is kept imprisoned in the space in the middle by intense magnetic fields.

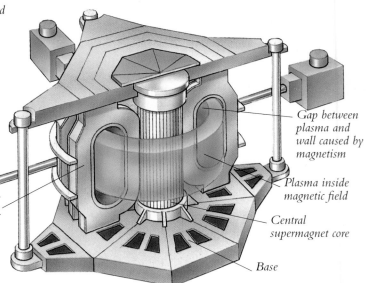

Gap between plasma and wall caused by magnetism

Plasma inside magnetic field

Supermagnetism in wall of ring-shaped plasma container

Central supermagnet core

Base

Launched into Space

A huge magnet-powered super gun could launch a satellite. It would have a very long barrel with powerful ring-shaped electromagnets at intervals along its length, switched on and off, one after the other. These would attract the satellite in its bullet casing, speed it up along the barrel, stage by stage, finally hurling it with amazing force and speed into Space.

Launcher with satellite or missile inside

Supermagnet ring switches on and off rapidly

Unmagnetized portion

Supermagnet rings come on and off one by one and pull the launcher at an ever increasing speed up the gun barrel

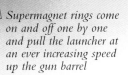

Helping the environment

Recycling is important, to save natural resources on Earth. Magnets and electromagnets help by sorting out metals and moving them around in the scrapyard, so that they can be melted down and reused.

More for less

Better designs of electromagnets help in many ways. In the generators of power stations, they can help to make more electricity using less fuel. Improved electromagnets in all kinds of machines use less electricity, yet produce more magnetism.

TRICKS WITH MAGNETS

M ANY amazing and magic-like tricks rely on the invisible power of magnets. For example, did you know you can easily remove paper-clips from water without getting your fingers wet, or that you can make a paper bat that hovers unsupported in mid air? These ideas are guaranteed to intrigue your friends. After learning about magnets in this book, you will probably be able to come up with lots more ideas of your own. Ask your friends, too, if they have any tricks that use the powers of simple magnets to such fascinating effect.

It is not difficult to do tricks with magnets, if you have the right materials handy.

M A T E R I A L S

You will need: paper-clips, beaker of water, magnet.

Fun with magnets

1 Put the paper-clips into the beaker of water. Place the magnet against the beaker's side. It should attract a paper-clip because magnetism is passing through the beaker.

2 Slowly slide the magnet up the side of the beaker. Do this carefully and the paper-clip will follow, attracted and dragged along by the magnet.

3 Keep sliding the magnet until it reaches the rim of the beaker. Now lift away the paper-clip. One by one do the same with the rest of the paper-clips.

M A T E R I A L S

You will need: black paper, white pencil, scissors, stiff green paper, sticky tape, stiff wire, paper-clips, string, strong magnet.

Bat magnet

1 Draw a large bat shape on to a sheet of black paper with the white pencil. Cut it out.

2 Tape stiff paper to the bat's underside, and stiff wire across the wings. Secure a piece of string.

3 Place several paper-clips on the paper used to stiffen the bat. Cover each clip with a piece of sticky tape to keep it secure.

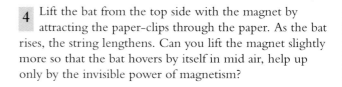

4 Lift the bat from the top side with the magnet by attracting the paper-clips through the paper. As the bat rises, the string lengthens. Can you lift the magnet slightly more so that the bat hovers by itself in mid air, help up only by the invisible power of magnetism?

INDEX

PICTURE CREDITS
b=bottom, t=top, c=centre, l=left, r=right
Bruce Coleman Ltd: J. Cancalosi 29bl. Cern Photo: 41tr. Hulton Getty Picture Collection Limited: 22tl. Marsell Collection: 29t, 29br. Marconi Wireless Telegraph Co. Ltd: 39t, 49tl. Mary Evans Picture Library: 10bl, 11tr, 11b. Science Museum: 38tl. Spacecharts: 30br. Tony Stone Images: K. Kelley 30bl, D. Fritts 31tl, L. Campbell 34t, M. Severns 35t, R. Planck 35br, C. Gupton 41bl, D. Smetzer 45bl, L. Duka 51bl, P. Cade 55bl, S. Johnson 56bl, C. Thatcher 61bl. Tony Stone Images/World Prescriptives: 31tr. Trip: B. Turner 5tl, H. Rogers 11tl, 40bl, 41tl, 43tl, 53br, J. Ringland 51br, B. Gibbs 58t. Zefa Pictures: 5b, 6t, 10br, 25all, 31b, 34br, 37b, 40br, 42ct, 45tr, 45br, 46bl, 47all, 57bl, 61cr.